I0846072

---

# "The Anti-Digital Product Digital Product Club" Guide

---

"THE ANTI-DIGITAL PRODUCT DIGITAL PRODUCT CLUB" GUIDE

Copyright © 2023

All rights reserved. No part of this publication may be reproduced, stored in a retrieval system, or transmitted in any form or by any means, whether electronic, mechanical photocopying, or recording, without the prior written permission of the publisher and author. All the information, exercises, techniques, skills, and concepts contained within this publication are of the nature of general comment only and are not in any way recommended as advice for individuals. The intention is to offer information that will provide a wider range of choices now and in the future, recognizing that we all have widely diverse circumstance and viewpoints. Should any reader choose to make use of the information contained herein, that is their decision and the contributors (and their companies), authors, and publishers do not assume any responsibility whatsoever under any condition or circumstances. It is recommended that the reader obtain his or her own advice.

# Unleash Your Digital Empire: A No-Nonsense Blueprint for Success

Welcome to "The Anti-Digital Product Digital Product Club Guide," where we strip away the fluff and dive straight into the heart of creating and selling digital products. This isn't just about information; it's about transformation. Are you ready to embark on a journey that will turn your passion into profit? Let's get started.

# CONTENTS

# CHAPTER ONE

## Introduction to the Digital Product Revolution

Welcome, visionary, to the dawn of the Digital Product Revolution! This chapter marks the beginning of your journey into the world of limitless possibilities and boundless wealth. Are you ready to unleash the power of the digital realm and transform your ideas into income? Let's dive right in.

### The Digital Product: A Game-Changer

In a world that's becoming increasingly digital, the concept of a digital product has become a game-changer. But what exactly is a digital product? It's a creation of your expertise, packaged in a format that can be delivered electronically. It could be an e-book, an online course, a downloadable software, an app, or any other digital offering. The magic lies in its scalability, flexibility, and potential for massive profit.

## Why Digital Products Matter

So, why should you care about digital products? First and foremost, they are the future of business. In an age where the online marketplace is thriving, digital products provide an unprecedented opportunity to monetize your knowledge, skills, and passions. Unlike physical products, digital ones have virtually no production or shipping costs, allowing you to keep a more significant portion of the revenue.

## A World of Opportunities

The digital realm offers a world of opportunities. Whether you're a seasoned expert in a particular field or a passionate individual with a unique perspective, there's a digital product waiting to be created by you. The beauty of this revolution is that it doesn't discriminate. It doesn't matter if you're an experienced entrepreneur or just starting out. It doesn't care about your age, background, or location. What matters is your determination, your creativity, and your readiness to seize the opportunities.

## Your Journey Starts Here

Your journey into the Digital Product Revolution starts right here, right now. Throughout this guide, we'll equip you with the knowledge, strategies, and inspiration needed to create and sell digital products. From creating your own unique products to leveraging Done-For-You (DFY) offerings, you'll explore every avenue to success. But remember, the revolution is not just about what you'll create; it's about the transformation you'll undergo.

The Digital Product Revolution is not a destination; it's a journey. It's a journey of self-discovery, innovation, and wealth creation. The digital world is your playground, and the possibilities are infinite. Are you ready to embrace this revolution? The time to act is now, and your journey starts with the turn of this page.

Stay tuned for the next chapters where we'll delve into the practical steps, strategies, and wisdom to navigate this revolution with confidence and conviction. Your digital empire awaits!

# CHAPTER TWO

## Getting Started in the Digital Product Arena

Welcome to Chapter 2 of your journey towards digital product success. It's time to roll up your sleeves and dive headfirst into the digital product arena. The digital landscape is your canvas, and your potential is limitless. Are you ready to take those crucial first steps? Let's begin your adventure.

### Defining the Digital Product Arena

Before we charge ahead, let's define the arena we're entering. The digital product arena encompasses a vast landscape filled with opportunities.

Here, you can create, market, and sell digital products that cater to various niches, needs, and passions. It's a world where you transform your knowledge, skills, and creativity into income.

## Your Path: Creator or Leverager

One of the first decisions you'll make is whether to be a Creator or a Leverager.

1. **Creator:** If you choose to be a Creator, you'll craft your digital products from scratch. This path allows you to unleash your creativity, turning your unique ideas into income. Whether it's an e-book, an online course, or digital artwork, you're the mastermind behind your creations.

2. **Leverager:** The Leverager path involves utilizing Done-For-You (DFY) products. You'll promote and sell existing digital products, saving you the time and effort required for creation. It's a faster entry into the digital product arena, where you'll earn commissions for sales.

## The Power of Your Niche

In the digital product arena, your niche is your guiding star. It's the space where your expertise, passion, and audience intersect. Your niche will determine the types of products you create or promote. The more you align with your niche, the more authentic and compelling your offerings become.

## Creating Your Digital Brand

Branding is your digital product's identity. It's the face of your business in the online world. Your brand tells a story, conveys a message, and builds trust with your audience. As you embark on this journey, remember that your brand should reflect your values, personality, and the essence of your digital products.

## Navigating the Digital Product Landscape

The digital product arena is a dynamic landscape with its own language, tools, and strategies. As you get started, be prepared to explore elements such as:

- **E-commerce Platforms:** Choose platforms that align with your goals, such as Shopify, WooCommerce, or ClickBank.

- **Payment Processing:** Set up secure payment gateways to handle transactions smoothly and reliably.

- **Content Management Systems:** Utilize systems like WordPress to create and manage your digital products.

- **Audience Building:** Start building your online presence through websites, social media, and email marketing.

## Your First Steps

Your journey begins with those initial, courageous steps. Whether you decide to create your products or leverage existing ones, the key is to start. Start planning, start creating, start promoting, and start learning. The digital product arena is a universe of opportunities, and every action you take brings you closer to success.

Stay tuned for the upcoming chapters where we'll explore more aspects of this exciting journey, from creating a powerful online presence to identifying the perfect digital products for your niche. Your digital empire starts here, and your potential is boundless. Are you ready to seize it?

# CHAPTER THREE

## Building Your Online Presence: Your Digital Storefront

Welcome to Chapter 3 of your journey to digital product success. Imagine your online presence as your digital storefront. Just as a physical storefront attracts customers, your online presence should captivate your audience. In this chapter, we'll explore how to create a digital storefront that leaves a lasting impression.

### Your Online Presence: Your Digital Storefront

Your online presence is more than just a website; it's the digital realm where your audience interacts with your brand. Think of it as your digital store, and it's crucial to make it inviting, trustworthy, and memorable.

## The Power of a Professional Website

In this digital age, your website is your central hub. It's the place where your audience learns about your digital products, your expertise, and your story. A professional website is like a well-kept store with clean windows, inviting displays, and a friendly salesperson to greet customers.

Your website should be user-friendly, responsive (mobile-friendly), and reflect your brand's personality. The goal is to build a seamless and engaging experience for your visitors.

## Navigational Simplicity

Your digital store should be easy to navigate. Consider a clear and intuitive menu that directs visitors to different sections, such as your products, blog, about page, and contact information. Make sure your visitors can find what they're looking for without frustration.

## High-Quality Content

Your digital storefront is more than just visuals; it's also about the content you offer. High-quality content adds value, educates, and engages your audience. Whether it's blog posts, videos, podcasts, or product descriptions, content should be relevant, informative, and well-presented.

## Trust-Building Elements

Trust is paramount in the digital world. Your store should include trust-building elements like customer testimonials, reviews, security certificates, and easy contact options. When visitors trust your store, they're more likely to make a purchase.

## The Beauty of Consistency

Consistency is the key to brand recognition. Your digital storefront should use consistent colors, fonts, and branding elements. This ensures that your audience instantly recognizes your store, whether they're on your website, social media, or in their email inbox.

## Search Engine Optimization (SEO)

If you want your digital store to shine in the vast online marketplace, you'll need to optimize it for search engines. SEO helps your website rank higher in search results, making it more accessible to potential customers.

## The Power of User Experience

User experience (UX) is vital. Your digital store should be designed with your audience in mind. It should load quickly, be easy to navigate, and provide an enjoyable experience. Think of it as a welcoming, well-lit store where everything is within reach.

## Building a Community

Your digital store is not just a one-way street; it's a place where you engage with your audience. Encourage comments, create discussion forums, and offer opportunities for your visitors to connect with each other. Building a community around your brand is a powerful way to boost engagement and loyalty.

## Remember, Your Store is Always Open

One of the beauties of a digital storefront is that it never closes. Your products are available 24/7, allowing you to reach customers from around the world. This means that while you sleep, your digital store can still make sales and grow your business.

As you embark on building your digital storefront, remember that it's a work in progress. Continuously improve and refine your online presence, just as you would with a physical store. Your digital empire starts with an inviting, trustworthy, and engaging online presence. Are you ready to create your digital storefront that beckons customers even while you sleep? Stay tuned for the upcoming chapters, where we'll explore finding profitable digital products and how to promote them effectively. Your journey to digital product success continues, and your potential knows no bounds.

# CHAPTER FOUR

## Finding Profitable Digital Products

Welcome to the chapter where we unearth the treasure troves of profitable digital products. In this digital product journey, success is not just about what you create; it's also about what you choose to offer to your audience. Let's dive into the art of finding digital products that turn your passion into profit.

### The Digital Product Ecosystem

The digital product ecosystem is vast and diverse, offering a myriad of opportunities. Your choice will depend on whether you aim to be a Creator or a Leverager.

1. **Creator:** If you're a Creator, you'll design your digital products from the ground up. This allows you to let your creativity run wild, producing unique offerings that cater to your niche.

2. **Leverager:** As a Leverager, you'll tap into the world of Done-For-You (DFY) products. This path is faster, as you'll promote and sell existing digital products created by others, earning a commission for every sale.

## Identifying Profitable Niches

Your journey begins by identifying profitable niches. A niche is a distinct segment of a larger market, characterized by its specific needs and interests. Here's how to find the niche that suits you:

1. **Passion and Knowledge:** Consider what you're passionate about and knowledgeable in. Your enthusiasm will shine through in your marketing efforts, making your products more compelling.

2. **Audience Needs:** Identify the problems or needs of your target audience. What solutions can you provide through your digital products?

3. **Competition Analysis:** Research your competitors in the chosen niche. Assess the demand and competition level to determine if it's a viable market.

## Digital Product Ideas

Now, let's brainstorm some digital product ideas:

- **E-books:** Create informative e-books on topics your audience is interested in.

- **Online Courses:** Develop comprehensive online courses on niche-specific subjects.

- **Digital Artwork:** If you have artistic talent, create digital artwork, illustrations, or graphics.

- **Software and Apps:** Design software or apps that simplify tasks or entertain.

- **Templates:** Craft templates for websites, social media, or documents.

- **Audio Products:** Record podcasts, music, or audiobooks.

- **Digital Photography:** If you're a photographer, sell your high-quality digital images.

## Leverage Done-For-You (DFY) Products

If you opt to be a Leverager, explore DFY products. These can include affiliate marketing programs, where you earn commissions by promoting other creators' products. Look for DFY products that align with your niche and offer genuine value to your audience.

## Validate Your Ideas

Before you dive into creation or promotion, validate your digital product ideas. This involves gauging demand and interest. You can conduct surveys, run pilot programs, or use social media to assess your audience's response.

## The Power of Testing

Don't forget the power of testing. When you create a new digital product, consider running small-scale tests before a full launch. Testing helps identify areas for improvement and refines your offerings.

## Your Next Steps

Your journey to finding profitable digital products is unfolding. Here are your next steps:

1. **Define Your Path:** Decide if you'll be a Creator or a Leverager.

2. **Choose Your Niche:** Identify a niche that aligns with your passion, expertise, and your audience's needs.

3. **Brainstorm Ideas:** Generate ideas for digital products you can create or promote.

4. **Validate and Test:** Ensure there's a demand for your chosen products through surveys and testing.

Remember, every step you take brings you closer to digital product success. Stay tuned for the upcoming chapters, where we'll delve into the art of promoting your digital products, creating high-quality content, and optimizing your online store. Your journey is in full swing, and the opportunities are boundless. Are you ready to make your digital product dreams a reality?

# CHAPTER FIVE

---

## Promoting Your Digital Products: The Art of Persuasion

Welcome to the exciting world of promotion! Now that you've chosen your digital products, it's time to shine a spotlight on them. This chapter is all about the art of persuasion, the magic that transforms a curious browser into a loyal customer.

## The Power of Persuasion

Persuasion is the heart and soul of marketing. It's the art of convincing, enticing, and engaging your audience in a way that moves them to take action. Whether you're a Creator or a Leverager, persuasion is your secret weapon.

## Know Your Audience

Effective persuasion starts with understanding your audience. Who are they? What do they need, desire, and fear? What problems can your digital product solve for them? By knowing your audience inside out, you can tailor your marketing efforts to speak directly to their hearts and minds.

## Captivating Content

Your content is your most potent persuasive tool. It's the bridge that connects your audience to your digital products. Create content that is:

- **Compelling:** Make your audience feel that they can't live without your product.

- **Informative:** Educate your audience about the value of your product.

- **Emotional:** Appeal to their emotions and show them how your product will improve their lives.

## Content Marketing

Content marketing is one of the most persuasive techniques. It involves creating valuable, informative content that attracts and engages your audience. This content can be in the form of blog posts, videos, infographics, or social media updates. Remember, it's not about selling; it's about adding value and building trust.

## Email Marketing

Your email list is a treasure chest of potential customers. Use email marketing to reach your audience directly, sharing valuable content, exclusive offers, and updates about your digital products. Craft compelling subject lines and captivating content to keep your subscribers eagerly awaiting your emails.

## The Power of Social Media

Social media platforms are your stage for showcasing your digital products. Use compelling visuals, engaging posts, and direct engagement with your audience to generate buzz around your offerings. Social media can help you build a community around your brand and foster authentic relationships with your customers.

## Paid Advertising

Paid advertising can be a game-changer. Platforms like Google Ads and Facebook Ads allow you to target specific audiences and reach potential customers who might not have found you otherwise. These ads can be particularly useful for promotion when you're just starting.

## Building Trust

Trust is the bedrock of persuasion. Your audience must trust your brand, your expertise, and your product's value. Ensure your digital storefront exudes trustworthiness, with customer testimonials, reviews, and secure payment options.

## Calls to Action (CTAs)

A compelling call to action is the final nudge that encourages your audience to take the desired action. Whether it's "Buy Now," "Sign Up," or "Download," your CTAs should be clear, eye-catching, and strategically placed.

## Measuring Success

The art of persuasion is an ongoing journey. To improve your persuasive techniques, you need to measure your efforts. Use analytics tools to track the performance of your marketing campaigns, emails, and social media posts. These insights will help you refine your strategy for even greater impact.

## Your Next Steps

As you venture into the art of persuasion, here are your next steps:

1. **Understand Your Audience:** Dive deep into your audience's desires and pain points.

2. **Create Compelling Content:** Develop content that speaks to your audience's heart and mind.

3. **Embrace Content Marketing:** Start creating valuable content that adds to your audience's knowledge.

4. **Harness Email Marketing:** Build and engage your email list.

5. **Leverage Social Media:** Use social platforms to create a community around your brand.

6. **Explore Paid Advertising:** Consider using paid advertising for wider reach.

7. **Focus on Building Trust:** Ensure your audience trusts your brand and your products.

8. **Master the Call to Action:** Create compelling CTAs that lead to action.

9. **Measure and Improve:** Continuously analyze your results and refine your persuasion techniques.

Your journey to digital product success is in full swing. In the upcoming chapters, we'll explore how to create high-quality content, optimize your digital storefront, and navigate the world of tracking and analytics. Your potential is boundless, and the art of persuasion is your path to turning curious visitors into dedicated customers. Are you ready to captivate and inspire?

# CHAPTER SIX

## Creating High-Quality Digital Content

Welcome to the chapter where we'll delve into the heart of your digital product business—creating high-quality content. Content is the soul of your digital products, and it's what sets you apart in a crowded digital landscape. Get ready to unleash your creativity and craft content that captivates, informs, and inspires.

## The Power of High-Quality Content

High-quality content is like a magnetic force. It attracts your audience, holds their attention, and converts them into loyal customers.

Whether you're a Creator or a Leverager, your content is your unique selling proposition.

## The Three Pillars of Quality Content

1. **Relevance:** Your content must be relevant to your niche and your audience's interests. It should address their pain points, desires, and questions. Think of your content as the solution they've been searching for.

2. **Value:** Every piece of content should add value to your audience's lives. It can inform, entertain, educate, or inspire. High-value content positions you as an authority in your niche.

3. **Engagement:** Engaging content captures your audience's attention and keeps them coming back for more. It should be interesting, interactive, and encourage your audience to take action.

## Content Types

Your digital product content can take various forms, depending on your niche and audience:

- **E-books:** Create comprehensive guides or informative e-books that solve specific problems or provide valuable information.

- **Online Courses:** Develop structured online courses that educate and empower your audience.

- **Blog Posts:** Regularly publish blog posts that address niche-related topics and showcase your expertise.

- **Videos:** Craft engaging video content, whether it's tutorials, vlogs, or product demonstrations.

- **Podcasts:** If audio is your forte, consider launching a podcast where you discuss relevant topics and invite industry experts.

## Creating High-Quality Content

1. **Research:** Understand your audience's needs and desires through market research. What questions do they have? What problems do they face? What solutions are they seeking?

2. **Planning:** Create a content strategy that outlines your topics, formats, and publishing schedule. A well-thought-out plan will keep your content organized and consistent.

3. **Originality:** Your content should stand out. Inject your unique perspective, experiences, and personality into every piece. Originality is what makes your content memorable.

4. **Clarity:** Ensure your content is clear and easy to understand. Use straightforward language, avoid jargon, and break down complex concepts into digestible chunks.

5. **Visual Appeal:** For visual content, such as videos and infographics, pay attention to aesthetics. Eye-catching visuals can make your content more engaging.

6. **Value-Oriented:** Every piece of content should offer something valuable to your audience. It could be information, entertainment, inspiration, or a combination of these.

7. **Consistency:** Consistency in content creation is vital. Regularly publish new content to keep your audience engaged and coming back for more.

## Quality Over Quantity

It's not about the quantity of content you produce, but the quality. A single piece of high-quality content can outperform a dozen mediocre ones. Focus on creating content that truly matters to your audience.

## Your Next Steps

As you embark on your content creation journey, here are your next steps:

1. **Understand Your Audience:** Know their needs, desires, and pain points.

2. **Plan Your Content:** Develop a content strategy that outlines your topics and publishing schedule.

3. **Inject Originality:** Make your content unique by infusing your perspective and personality.

4. **Prioritize Clarity:** Ensure your content is easy to understand.

5. **Visual Appeal:** If applicable, enhance the visual appeal of your content.

6. **Deliver Value: Ensure** each piece of content adds value to your audience.

7. **Maintain Consistency:** Stick to a consistent publishing schedule.

Your journey to creating high-quality content is about to set sail. Stay tuned for the upcoming chapters, where we'll explore the art of tracking and analytics, compliance, and the crucial elements of scaling your digital product empire. Your potential is limitless, and your content is your vessel to reach it. Are you ready to craft content that inspires and transforms lives?

# CHAPTER SEVEN

---

## Tracking and Analytics: The Data-Driven Advantage

Welcome to the chapter where we transform data into power. In this digital age, information is your greatest ally. Tracking and analytics are your compass, guiding you towards success. Get ready to harness the incredible data-driven advantage on your journey.

### The Power of Data

Data is the fuel that powers your digital product empire. It tells you what's working, what's not, and where you can improve. It's not just numbers and charts; it's the roadmap to your success.

## What to Track

1. **Website Traffic:** Monitor the number of visitors, page views, and bounce rate on your digital storefront. Understand where your traffic is coming from (e.g., social media, search engines) to optimize your strategies.

2. **Conversion Rates:** Track how many visitors take the desired actions, such as signing up for your email list, making a purchase, or downloading a lead magnet.

3. **Email Campaign Performance:** Analyze open rates, click-through rates, and conversion rates for your email marketing campaigns.

4. **Social Media Metrics:** Keep an eye on engagement metrics on social platforms, such as likes, shares, comments, and follower growth.

5. **Content Performance:** Identify which content pieces are resonating with your audience and driving the most engagement.

6. **Sales Data:** Keep detailed records of your product sales, including revenue, customer demographics, and refund rates.

## Tools for Tracking

There are several tools and platforms that can help you track and analyze your digital product performance:

- **Google Analytics:** A powerful tool for tracking website data, traffic sources, and user behavior.

- **Email Marketing Analytics:** Email marketing platforms provide data on open rates, click-through rates, and subscriber activity.

- **Social Media Insights:** Each social platform offers insights and analytics for business accounts.

- **E-commerce Platforms:** If you're selling digital products, your e-commerce platform may provide sales data and customer insights.

- **Content Management Systems:** CMS like WordPress often have built-in analytics or offer plugins for tracking website data.

## The Analytics Advantage

Understanding your data is where the advantage lies:

- **Optimization:** Data helps you identify areas of improvement. It tells you what's working and what's not, allowing you to optimize your strategies.

- **Audience Insights:** Analyzing data reveals valuable insights about your audience's behavior and preferences.

- **Personalization:** With data, you can personalize your marketing and content to cater to specific segments of your audience.

- **Cost-Efficiency:** Data allows you to allocate your budget where it matters most, avoiding wasted resources.

- **Data-Driven Decisions:** Instead of making decisions based on assumptions, you can make informed choices backed by data.

## The Continuous Cycle

Tracking and analytics are not a one-time affair. It's a continuous cycle of data collection, analysis, optimization, and then starting the cycle again. The more you engage in this process, the sharper your strategies become.

## Your Next Steps

As you embark on your data-driven journey, here are your next steps:

1. **Identify What to Track:** Determine which metrics are most relevant to your digital product business.

2. **Select Tracking Tools:** Choose the tools and platforms that will help you collect the necessary data.

3. **Start Tracking:** Begin collecting data on your website, email marketing, social media, and sales.

4. **Analyze the Data:** Regularly review your data to gain insights and identify areas for improvement.

5. **Optimize Your Strategies:** Use the insights from your data to optimize your digital product marketing and content.

Your journey to data-driven success is underway. Stay tuned for the upcoming chapters, where we'll explore compliance and legal considerations, scaling your digital product empire, and common mistakes to avoid. Your potential is limitless, and your data is your compass. Are you ready to harness the data-driven advantage and navigate the path to success?

# CHAPTER EIGHT

## Compliance and Legal Considerations

Welcome to the chapter where we delve into the essential topic of compliance and legal considerations in your digital product journey. Just as a ship must navigate treacherous waters, your business must sail the legal seas with knowledge and care. Let's ensure your empire is built on solid, compliant ground.

## The Legal Framework

The digital product world, like any other business realm, has a legal framework. Understanding and complying with these regulations is essential for your success. Here are some key areas to consider:

1. **Business Structure:** Depending on your location and goals, you may need to choose the right business structure, such as sole proprietorship, LLC, or corporation.

2. **Intellectual Property:** Protect your intellectual property through copyrights, trademarks, and patents. Ensure your products don't infringe on others' intellectual property rights.

3. **Terms of Service and Privacy Policies:** Create clear terms of service and privacy policies for your website and digital products. These documents outline the rules for using your products and how you handle user data.

4. **Consumer Protection Laws:** Understand consumer protection laws and regulations in your region. This includes providing accurate product information and handling refunds or disputes.

5. **Taxation:** Be aware of tax obligations and requirements, including sales tax and income tax.

6. **Affiliate Marketing Regulations:** If you engage in affiliate marketing, understand the regulations and disclosure requirements in **your area.**

7. **Compliance with Payment Processors:** Ensure that your payment processing and e-commerce systems comply with industry standards and financial regulations.

## Data Security

Data security is paramount. If you collect and store user data, you must protect it. Understand data protection laws such as the General Data Protection Regulation (GDPR) and implement necessary security measures.

## Contractual Agreements

When working with affiliates, collaborators, or third-party providers, it's crucial to have clear contractual agreements in place. Contracts should outline responsibilities, payment terms, and dispute resolution procedures.

## Accessibility

Digital products should be accessible to all, including individuals with disabilities. Ensure that your products meet accessibility standards to comply with accessibility laws like the Americans with Disabilities Act (ADA).

## Keep Records

Documentation is your safeguard. Maintain thorough records of your business activities, financial transactions, contracts, and compliance efforts. These records are essential in case of legal issues or audits.

## Seek Legal Advice

While you can educate yourself on legal matters, seeking legal advice from an attorney experienced in digital business can save you from costly mistakes. A legal expert can provide guidance tailored to your specific situation.

## Your Next Steps

As you navigate the legal seas, here are your next steps:

1. **Understand Legal Requirements:** Educate yourself about the legal regulations relevant to your digital product business.

2. **Implement Legal Documents:** Create essential legal documents, including terms of service, privacy policies, and contracts.

3. **Secure Data:** Ensure data security measures are in place to protect user information.

4. **Comply with Accessibility Standards:** Make your digital products accessible to all.

5. **Maintain Records:** Keep detailed records of your business activities and compliance efforts.

6. **Seek Legal Advice:** Consult with an attorney experienced in digital business for personalized guidance.

Your journey to digital product success is now fortified with legal knowledge. Stay tuned for the upcoming chapters, where we'll explore scaling your digital product empire and common mistakes to avoid. Your empire's foundations are strong, and you're ready to navigate the legal waters with confidence. Are you prepared to sail ahead?

# CHAPTER NINE

## Scaling Your Digital Product Empire

Welcome to the chapter that's all about expansion and growth. It's time to take your digital product empire to the next level. Just as a tree grows, your business can too, reaching new heights. Let's explore how to scale your empire, expand your influence, and achieve your dreams.

## The Power of Scaling

Scaling your digital product business means increasing your reach, revenue, and impact. It's the moment you step into the big league, but it requires a strategic approach.

## 1. Streamlined Processes

Efficiency is your best friend when scaling. Streamline your processes to save time and resources. Invest in automation tools to handle repetitive tasks, manage customer inquiries, and keep your operations running smoothly.

## 2. Expand Your Product Line

Diversify your digital product offerings. Consider creating new products or offering complementary ones. Expanding your product line not only broadens your reach but also keeps existing customers engaged.

## 3. Target New Markets

Look beyond your current market. Explore new niches and demographics that could benefit from your products. Research your target audience thoroughly and adapt your marketing to their needs and preferences.

## 4. Collaborate and Outsource

Don't be afraid to collaborate with experts or outsource tasks that are not your strengths. Partnering with other entrepreneurs can open doors to new opportunities, while outsourcing allows you to focus on what you do best.

## 5. Marketing Strategies

Your marketing efforts should evolve as you scale. Invest in paid advertising, influencer marketing, and affiliate partnerships to increase your visibility. Craft a comprehensive marketing plan that aligns with your growth goals.

## 6. Customer Support

Maintain excellent customer support even as you scale. Happy customers are your best brand ambassadors. Offer efficient support channels and continue to listen to their feedback.

## 7. Financial Planning

Scaling requires investment. Carefully plan your finances, budget for growth, and ensure you have the necessary capital to support your expansion.

## 8. Monitor Performance

As you scale, tracking and analytics become even more critical. Regularly evaluate your strategies, monitor your key performance indicators, and adjust your tactics based on what works best.

## 9. Training and Development

Invest in your team's training and development. Equip them with the skills and knowledge needed to support your growing business.

## 10. Stay Agile

While scaling is about growth, it's essential to remain agile. Be ready to adapt and pivot based on market changes and evolving customer needs.

## Your Next Steps

As you set sail on your scaling journey, here are your next steps:

1. **Streamline Processes:** Identify areas for efficiency improvements and consider automation tools.

2. **Expand Your Product Line:** Explore new digital products or complementary offerings.

3. **Target New Markets:** Research and reach out to new niches and demographics.

4. **Collaborate and Outsource:** Partner with experts and outsource non-core tasks.

5. **Revamp Marketing:** Invest in new marketing strategies that align with your growth goals.

6. **Prioritize Customer Support:** Continue to offer excellent customer support.

7. **Financial Planning:** Plan your finances and budget for growth.

8. **Monitor Performance:** Regularly evaluate your strategies and adapt.

9. **Training and Development:** Invest in your team's skills and knowledge.

10. **Stay Agile:** Be ready to adapt to market changes and evolving customer needs.

Your journey to scaling your digital product empire has begun. Stay tuned for the final chapter, where we'll explore common mistakes to avoid. You're on the cusp of great expansion, and your potential knows no bounds. Are you prepared to scale your empire to new heights?

# CHAPTER TEN

## Common Digital Product Mistakes to Avoid

Welcome to the final chapter of your incredible journey in the digital product realm. It's a chapter of enlightenment, where we'll navigate through the common pitfalls and mistakes made by many. Knowing what to avoid is as crucial as knowing what to embrace. Let's uncover these mistakes, so you can steer clear and keep your empire on a course for success.

## Embracing Failure as a Teacher

Mistakes are not the end; they're the beginning. In the digital product world, mistakes can be profound lessons, like a ship learning from rough waters. Let's explore some of the most common mistakes and how to navigate around them:

## 1. Neglecting Market Research

Some entrepreneurs rush into creating digital products without understanding their market. It's like setting sail without a map. Market research is your compass, guiding you towards your audience's needs, preferences, and pain points.

## 2. Poor Product Quality

Quality is your flagship. Cutting corners on product quality can sink your business faster than a storm at sea. Always prioritize delivering value and excellence to your customers.

## 3. Neglecting Customer Feedback

Customer feedback is your North Star. Ignoring it is like sailing blind. Continuously listen to your customers, adapt to their feedback, and improve your products and services.

## 4. Overlooking Legalities

Failing to comply with legal regulations can be like hitting a hidden rock. Stay informed about the legal requirements in your industry and region. Seek legal advice when needed and ensure your business is on solid legal ground.

## 5. Mismanaged Finances

Money is your lifeline. Poor financial management can leave you stranded. Keep a close eye on your finances, budget wisely, and plan for growth with a sound financial strategy.

## 6. Ineffective Marketing

Ineffective marketing can be like hoisting a sail without the wind. Invest in marketing strategies that align with your goals. Don't be afraid to pivot and experiment with new approaches.

## 7. Lack of Customer Support

A ship without a crew is directionless. Failing to provide excellent customer support can lead to lost customers. Prioritize support to keep your customers satisfied and loyal.

## 8. Ignoring Data

Data is your guide. Neglecting analytics is like navigating without a compass. Regularly analyze your data, track your performance, and use these insights to steer your business in the right direction.

## 9. Resistance to Change

In the dynamic digital world, resistance to change can be your anchor. Stay agile, adapt to market shifts, and be open to new opportunities.

## 10. Not Learning from Failure

The most significant mistake is not learning from your failures. Failure is not a setback; it's a lesson. Embrace it, adjust your course, and keep moving forward.

## Your Next Steps

As you embark on this final leg of your journey, remember these next steps:

1. **Embrace Failure:** Treat mistakes as valuable lessons.

2. **Prioritize Market Research:** Understand your audience and their needs.

3. **Deliver Quality:** Maintain high standards in product quality.

4. **Listen to Customers:** Continuously gather and act on customer feedback.

5. **Stay Compliant:** Be aware of and adhere to legal regulations.

6. **Manage Finances:** Keep a close eye on your financial health.

7. **Optimize Marketing:** Invest in effective marketing strategies.

8. **Prioritize Customer Support:** Offer excellent support to keep customers happy.

9. **Leverage Data:** Regularly analyze your data for insights.

10. **Embrace Change:** Stay adaptable and open to new opportunities.

Your journey through the digital product world is coming to a close, but it's just the beginning of an exciting adventure. With the knowledge gained from these chapters, you're ready to set sail, avoid the common mistakes, and steer your empire towards success. Are you prepared to journey onward?

# CHAPTER ELEVEN

## Success Stories and Inspirations

Welcome to the chapter that's bound to inspire and ignite your entrepreneurial spirit. Here, we're not just looking at success; we're celebrating it. By exploring the journeys and stories of those who have walked this path before you, you'll see that success is not a distant island but a tangible destination. Let's dive into the deep sea of success stories and find inspiration to fuel your own journey.

## The Power of Inspiration

Success stories aren't just tales of achievement; they're wellsprings of inspiration. They show you what's possible and prove that dreams can become realities. In this chapter, you'll meet individuals who dared to dream, took action, and turned their digital product ventures into success stories.

## Story 1: The Content Creator Extraordinaire

Meet Sarah, a content creator who started with a simple blog. She shared her passion and expertise, growing her audience over time. She soon realized the potential of digital products. Sarah created e-books, courses, and digital downloads. Today, she not only inspires others but generates a substantial income doing what she loves.

**Lesson:** Sarah's story reminds us that passion and consistency can lead to remarkable success. Share your knowledge, and your audience will grow.

## Story 2: The Savvy Affiliate Marketer

Say hello to Alex, who began as an affiliate marketer in the wealth niche. With dedicated effort, he built a loyal following through blogs, social media, and email marketing. Alex didn't stop there. He expanded into creating his digital products, offering financial advice and tools. Today, he's a prominent figure in the digital wealth space.

**Lesson:** Alex's journey teaches us the power of building expertise and credibility, which can evolve into a thriving business.

## Story 3: The Innovator

Meet Emily, a creative thinker. She identified a gap in the market and developed a digital product that solved a specific problem. Through diligent marketing and strong customer support, Emily's product gained traction. Her innovation not only improved lives but also became a sustainable income source.

**Lesson:** Emily's story reminds us that identifying unmet needs and crafting solutions can be the key to success.

## Story 4: The Resilient Scaling Expert

John began his journey as a solo entrepreneur. His digital product empire grew rapidly, but he faced challenges along the way. John didn't let obstacles deter him; instead, he sought knowledge, built a talented team, and continued to scale his business.

**Lesson:** John's story demonstrates the power of resilience, adaptability, and the importance of surrounding yourself with a strong support system.

## Story 5: The Game-Changer

Meet Maria, a visionary who revolutionized her industry. She introduced a unique digital product that disrupted the market. Maria's innovation not only changed the way people interacted with her niche but also brought substantial financial success

**Lesson:** Maria's journey shows that daring to be different and introducing groundbreaking ideas can lead to unparalleled success.

## Your Next Steps

As you immerse yourself in these stories, remember the following steps to shape your own success story:

1. **Embrace Passion:** Pursue your passions, and you'll find the energy to persist.

2. **Build Expertise:** Share your knowledge and build your credibility in your niche.

3. **Innovate:** Seek opportunities to address unmet needs and develop unique solutions.

4. **Resilience:** Persevere through challenges and seek support when needed.

5. **Dare to Be Different:** Don't be afraid to introduce new and groundbreaking ideas.

Your journey in the world of digital products is a story waiting to be written. These stories are not distant galaxies; they're constellations of inspiration, lighting your path towards your own achievements. The final chapter of this guide has set you on a course to your own success story. Are you ready to pen the next chapter?

# CHAPTER TWELVE

## Conclusion and Next Steps

Congratulations on completing this incredible journey through the world of digital products! You've acquired a treasure trove of knowledge, inspiration, and strategies to embark on your own adventure. As we conclude this guide, let's chart a course for your next steps, ensuring you're ready to set sail on your path to digital product success.

## The Closing of One Chapter, the Beginning of Another

Just as a chapter ends, another begins. Your journey in the world of digital products has just started. Let's take a moment to reflect on your achievements and prepare for the path ahead.

## Reflect on Your Journey

Pause and reflect on what you've learned. You've gained insights into affiliate marketing, digital product creation, scaling your business, and the pitfalls to avoid. You've been inspired by success stories and equipped with the tools to make your own mark.

## Celebrate Your Progress

Celebrate your progress and the steps you've taken. Success is not just the destination; it's every milestone along the way. You've already achieved more than you may realize.

## Setting Your Sails for Success

Now, let's focus on your next steps. Your journey has only just begun, and there's a world of opportunity waiting for you.

## 1. Take Action

Action is the wind that propels your ship forward. Don't wait for the perfect moment; the perfect moment is now. Start applying the knowledge and strategies you've gained.

## 2. Set Clear Goals

Define your goals and objectives. Where do you want to be in six months, a year, or five years? Having clear goals will guide your efforts and keep you on track.

## 3. Continual Learning

The digital landscape is always changing. Stay curious and never stop learning. Seek out new information, strategies, and trends to keep your business innovative.

## 4. Network and Collaborate

You don't have to sail this journey alone. Connect with like-minded individuals, mentors, and potential collaborators. Networking can open doors to new opportunities.

## 5. Test and Adapt

Digital product success often requires experimentation. Test different strategies and be willing to adapt based on what works best for your business.

## 6. Monitor and Optimize

Regularly analyze your data and performance. Use the insights to optimize your strategies, products, and marketing efforts.

## 7. Seek Support

If you encounter challenges, seek support from peers, mentors, or professionals. You're not expected to have all the answers; the digital world is vast and ever-evolving.

## 8. Persevere

Your journey may have moments of uncertainty or rough seas, but remember, every successful explorer faced challenges. Perseverance is your anchor in turbulent times.

## Your Journey Awaits

As we conclude this guide, remember that your journey is unique. The knowledge and inspiration you've gained here are your compass, but you are the captain of your ship. Your potential is boundless, your dreams within reach, and your success is only limited by your determination and action.

So, set your sails, embrace the journey, and chase your dreams. The digital world is vast, but you are ready to navigate it. Are you prepared to embark on the incredible journey that awaits? Your voyage is about to begin.

# "The Only Time is Now"

Congratulations on completing this life-altering journey through "The Anti-Digital Product Digital Product Club" Guide. You've absorbed a wealth of knowledge, stoked the fires of inspiration, and now, you stand at the crossroads of your dreams and are ready for the blueprint.

As you reflect on your path, it's essential to remember that your journey to financial freedom is not just a wish; it's a commitment. Your dreams and goals are within your grasp, and now it's time to take the next steps to make them a reality.

Imagine a life where you're not working to make a living but living life to the fullest. Where you set the course of your destiny, and your financial worries become a thing of the past

This is where "From Idea to Income: The Anti-Digital Product Digital Product Blueprint" comes into play. This course is the gateway to diving deeper into what you need to get started on your path to financial freedom. It's the key to unlock the doors of possibilities that await you.

Here's the magic: "From Idea to Income" not only offers comprehensive insights, but it also provides all the resources, tips, and guidance that competitors would charge you thousands for. It's your secret treasure chest of wisdom, waiting for you to claim.

You see, your dreams are not just fantasies; they're a calling, and this course is your answer. So, take the next step, commit to your success, and open the doors to your financial freedom.

Remember, the future you desire is not in the distance; it's right here, waiting for you to claim it. "From Idea to Income" is your bridge to that future. You're just one decision away from living the life you've always envisioned. So don't wait; seize the opportunity now. Click on the link below to get your hands on "From Idea to Income" and take the next giant leap towards your dreams. Your success story is waiting to be written, and this book is your pen and paper.

**[Click here to purchase "From Idea to Income:**

**The Anti-Digital Product Digital Product Blueprint"]**

**https://stan.store/eklektikdigital**

Are you ready to seize your dreams, command your destiny, and embark on the journey to financial freedom? Your adventure awaits, and "From Idea to Income" is your compass. Let's set sail towards the life you've always wanted.

www.ingramcontent.com/pod-product-compliance
Lightning Source LLC
Chambersburg PA
CBHW060845260726
48661CB00002B/613